THE NATURAL WONDERS OF
CANADA

CLB 1954
This edition published by Bramley Books 1988.
© 1988 Colour Library Books Ltd, Godalming, Surrey, England.
All rights reserved.
Printed and bound in Barcelona, Spain, by Cronion, S.A.
ISBN 0 86283 646 8

THE NATURAL WONDERS OF
CANADA

Text by Andrea C. Le Coq

BRAMLEY BOOKS

In Canada, the moving and majestic music of nature can be heard in the thrust of waterfalls, the rush of chinook winds, in bubbling, roaring rapids and in the golden silence of remote wilderness. These sounds, a veritable symphony whose only conductor is God, create magnificent music in a land far beyond the reach of human hands. The harmony in Canada comes not from the voice of technological advancement, but from the primal controlling force in the universe – nature.

The geographic splendors that Canada embraces are perfect designs of environmental integrity, captivating and awesome in their functional and decorative operation. Never static, and seemingly indestructible, the wonders of Canada strike a balance in accordance with their polarity and their unity.

The names assigned to Canada's natural phenomena, as evidenced in the language of rivers, canyons, mountains and lakes, are derived from all things natural, as are the myriad materials, foods, fabrics and chemicals we use in everyday life. There is Porcupine Plain, Otter Lake, Easygoing Creek, Beehive Creek, Great Beaver Lake, Fallen Timber River, Crowsnest Forest, Pine Rapids and Sheep Mountain. All of these words communicate the meaning of Canada and reflect the bounty that thrives within her boundaries.

The metaphors and symbols of Canada's language and spirit are drawn, too, from Indian beliefs and inspirations. The Indians who inhabited this sacred and virgin land were at one with nature, at peace with its ever-vibrating pulse and, perhaps more than any group of people, they respected and worshipped earthly and celestial gifts. Canada is, therefore, blessed with an aura of the almighty and bestowed with a sense of purity that can never be violated.

Canada is the second largest country in the world. With an area of 3,845,744 square miles, it is as diverse as it is unique. Both gentle and rugged, Canada is composed of spectacular mountains and level plains, near deserts and glacial tundra, deep forests and fertile farmland, fishing villages and sophisticated cities. It is a land worth exploring intensively, even though it is unlikely that anyone could ever know it in its entirety.

Canada is a rich domain of forests, plains, rivers, lakes and the spreading northland. Discovered and developed by people who had to cope with the outdoors, there was always the struggle of distance, rocks, trees, water, heat and cold, break-up, freeze-up, blackflies and swamps. Someone always had to know how to navigate the canoes, light the campfire, blaze the trail and hunt for food. Although little has been changed by "accessibility," the transportation used today could eventually pose a threat to the fragile ecosystem. The tools used today range from float and bush planes, tractors and bulldozers to dynamite, diamond drills and snowmobiles. These have enabled Canada to become developed in a manner that would have astounded the men who "pushed the Canadian Pacific Railway across the prairies." But Canada is a vast country and still very much an unspoiled frontier.

Canada's ten provinces and two territories stretch over 4,000 miles from the capes of Newfoundland on the Atlantic to the Queen Charlotte Islands in the Pacific, and almost 3,000 miles from the temperate Great Lakes to Cape Columbia on Ellesmere Island, within 500 miles of the North Pole. All across Canada, enormous woodlands, thriving bird and animal life, high alpine meadows and hidden lakes are protected by law, but also by their extreme remoteness. The rough gravel roads into some of the choicest spots are for the intrepid, as are the canoe routes that must be followed to penetrate beyond the fringes of other areas.

From Lake Superior to the Rockies lies the huge expanse of the Canadian Prairies. Manitoba, Saskatchewan and Alberta are among the areas of the civilized world least worried about the population explosion. There is one square mile for every five of the 3,350,000 people in those provinces. And the gradual movement of half of them into the half dozen largest cities leaves the prairie country lonelier than it was a hundred years ago, when the Indians pursued great herds of roaming buffaloes.

Because of the myriad lakes, the Europeans were able to forge westward in adventuresome, curious and rapacious spirit. The Great Lakes drainage area, stretching from James Bay almost to New York City, is nearly as big as Britain and France combined, and is one of the most heavily industrialized regions on earth. The ecological balance of Canada can be disrupted, so it is with great caution that its provinces must continue to develop its resources. To a large degree, Canada is as populous as it is because the Great Lakes were there to carry the population spill of Europe westward in the 18th and 19th centuries. But today, along the 1,800 miles of navigable water from Lake Superior to the mouth of the St. Lawrence, there are countless signs that mankind has abused the lakes as well as used them.

Lake Superior, which covers 32,483 square miles, remains relatively unscathed because of the small population living near it. But the other lakes are all suffering. In the past decade, Canada has passed a flurry of legislation designed to halt the destruction, and billions of dollars have been allocated to repair the damage caused by human and industrial effluent. There are, however, some good signs to indicate that this concern is not too late.

The Great Lakes are so vast that they are really inland seas. Of all the world's landlocked bodies of water, only the Caspian Sea is bigger than Lake Superior, the last of the Great Lakes to be created following the last ice age, 10,000 years ago. Canada is lakes. As glaciers retreated, the land began to rise again. Crags, fissures and strange rock formations appeared, some of them mountainous deposits of rock and earth that had been suspended in ice for centuries, others the relics of weather-beaten mountains perhaps 600 million years old.

Physical disruptions such as glaciers, volcanoes and earthquakes have carved enormous valleys. When the glaciers had melted, they filled deep lakes that now cover about 7.6 percent of Canada with about 15 percent of the world's fresh water. There are nine Canadian lakes over 100 miles long and 35 others more than 50 miles long. Great Bear Lake, Great Slave Lake and Lake Winnipeg, for instance, cover 12,275, 10,980 and 9,465 square miles respectively, and are larger than some of the Great Lakes. In other millenia, volcanoes and earthquakes pushed vast mountain ranges up out of the earth. In still others, erosion and glaciation compressed and contorted older mountains.

The legacy of Canada's glaciers is a massive diversity of terrain, wildlife, climate and vegetation. Before railways and roads served every community, the lakes were the only way to reach many communities, especially new settlements that grew almost overnight as new sources of mineral wealth were discovered.

These physical disruptions have left Canada with five distinctive geographical regions, each with its own characteristic features and attractions. These five regions are Atlantic Canada, which encompasses Newfoundland, Labrador, Nova Scotia, Prince Edward Island and New Brunswick. Eastern Canada envelops Ontario and Quebec. Central Canada includes Saskatchewan and Manitoba. Western Canada includes British Columbia and Alberta, and northern Canada embodies the Yukon and the Northwest Territories.

So many things are part of Canada's natural heritage. Canada has inexhaustible resources of water, and also has oil, minerals, metals and trees. Canada's underground riches are still keeping prospectors busy, although these days they explore by bush plane, expecially in the gold, silver and uranium mining area of northeastern Ontario, where the gold is in streams and rivers rather than underground. Extremely rich gold mines on the headwaters of the Yukon, extensive areas of gold, copper and silver ore in the mountain regions of British Columbia, immense coal deposits in the Crowsnest Pass and on the prairies, and veins of silver and cobalt of extraordinary richness in Northern Ontario all deeply affected the industrial condition of Canada and illustrate the vastness of its undeveloped resources.

What is probably the richest vein of silver ever found stretches vertically down from a droplet of land called Silver Island in Lake Superior's Thunder Bay. Almost a century ago, silver worth millions of dollars was mined there before the shaft reached a depth of 1,300 feet and it proved impossible to keep the lake water out.

Next to agriculture, lumbering is the major industry, supplying building materials and fuel, and providing pulp for newsprint mills in Canada and abroad. The large number of trees now being cut down is depleting many forests and the eco system is threatened unless the trees are replaced.

In spite of great improvidence, and loss by fire, the forest wealth of Canada is still the greatest in the world. Measures have been taken, both by provincial and federal governments, for its preservation, and for reafforestation of depleted areas. Certain provinces prohibit the exportation of logs to the United States.

The national parks of Canada are dedicated to the protection of wildlife and to the preservation of our natural environment. The national park system in Canada started in 1885, when an area of ten square miles was set aside at Banff to protect the mineral hot springs on Sulphur Mountain from uncontrolled commercial exploitation. This park has grown to an area of 2,500 square miles and is flanked by Jasper National Park, one of the biggest wildlife and recreational parks in the world, with an area of 4,200 square miles.

This vast park system, with a total area in excess of 50,000 square miles, is supplemented by the provincial parks found in every province. The parks feature unusual natural phenomena. Glacier National Park in the Selkirk Mountains of southwestern British Columbia is magnificent. In Alberta, Waterton Lakes National Park manages to include plants and flowers from both the prairies and the Rocky Mountains and is also a noted wildlife sanctuary. Red Rock Canyon, deep in Waterton Lakes Park, is equally as spectacular.

The remote high country regions of the Yukon and Northwest Territories, as well as Canada's other provinces, are a botanist's paradise, with many as yet unidentified plants awaiting classification. Fields of brilliant wildflowers, such as poppies and blue lapine, carpet the tundra and meadows in a colorful display of delicate wonder. The great northern plains become arctic rock gardens bursting with millions of brightly colored lichens in the summer, and wild flowers such as poppy, cotton grass, mountain heather, arctic crocus, purple saxifrage, white heather and rhododendron.

The autumn-red maple leaf has been adopted by Canada as its emblem, but each of Canada's provinces has an official flower. Ten species of maple are native to Canada, but only two, the sugar maple and the black maple, have brilliant red leaves in autumn. These two species are found mainly in Ontario, Quebec and the Maritime Provinces. Both are tapped for syrup in the spring. For early settlers they were for many years the only source of sugar. Maples also provided the early colonists with wood for their houses and furniture.

There is a park to suit every taste, be it for fishing, bird-watching, botany, photography or solitary relaxation close to nature.

Sweeping east and south across the top of Canada are the remote wilderness expanses of the Yukon and Northwest Territories. These two territories comprise one of North America's last great outdoor frontiers. From the barren lands and polar bear grounds of the Arctic Ocean this area spreads across thousands of square miles of tundra, permafrost and stunted dwarf forests of spruce, pine, and muskeg. The north is broken by wild, brawling rivers, huge lakes surrounded by the ancient cliffs and rock outcroppings of the Canadian Shield, and spotted by a vast mosaic of countless small lakes and ponds. The Northwest Territories form a vast wilderness of 1.4 million square miles, while the Yukon takes in 207,076 square miles.

Observed from a bush plane, the barren ground of northern Canada appears to be a mosaic of lakes and rivers wrought by the ebb and flow of great ice sheets, with desolate tundra covered with boulders and thick carpets of caribou moss. Tundra pools, or kettle ponds, discoloured by organic stains of sepia and copper, are famous breeding grounds for ducks, geese and wading birds. The dry rock tundra is the habitat of northern grouse, or ptarmigan, and snowy owls which nest in the grass flats, along with rough-legged hawks, peregrine falcons, gray jays, tufted puffins and ravens. Butterflies, bees, arctic fox, wolves and the orange-colored ground squirrel also thrive in these areas.

One of the most profound sights in the far north is the mysterious herds of migrating caribou, drifting "like grayish-white specters across the taiga of the barren lands on their annual trek to the treeline, the land of lichen, in a phenomenon known as the 'throng' moving in seemingly endless single filelines along deeply furrowed trails often no more than 6-12 inches wide. They go in search of browse such as berry bushes and birch, and the thick white lichen, sometimes more than two feet thick, that forms a rumpled carpet on the tundra during the spring and summer months."

Kluane National Park and the great St. Elias Mountains offer some of the most spectacular high peaks in the world. Mount Logan, at 19,850 feet, towers over a dozen other peaks above 10,000 feet. Mountaineers from around the world use the St. Elias peaks as a final training ground before taking on the great peaks of the Himalayas.

The hundreds of wild rivers in the Yukon plunge down from the high glacial peaks of the St. Elias Mountains and Mackenzie Mountains and flow through moose pastures and dense, evergreen Boreal forests, past rotting, abandoned gold-rush settlements into the land of the beaver, wolverine and caribou. Wolf, coyote, red fox, lynx, otter and snowshoe hare are found throughout the Boreal forest area of Kluane National Park. Dall sheep and mountain goats roam the rocky slopes and cliffs of Sheep Mountain and the highlands in the south.

Baffin Island National Park, the first national park above the Arctic Circle, is full of long, narrow fjords, glacier-filled mountain valleys and a massive icecap that makes this 8,290-square-mile park one of Canada's most spectacular. The cliffs of some fjords tower 3,000 feet above the sea. Dominating the highlands, where mountains reach 7,000 feet, is Penny Ice Cap. Largest of the glaciers extending from the 2,200 square mile cap is Coronation Glacier, 20 miles long and two miles wide. Whale, seal and walrus are found in the fjords, and land mammals include polar bear, arctic fox and caribou. The Canada goose, snowy owl, rare gyrfalcon and whistling swan are among 40 species of birds in the park. Wood Buffalo National Park, with 17,300 square miles, is the largest national park in the world, and provides a haven for about 8,000 bison and about fifty of the nearly extinct whooping crane.

Canada's western provinces, British Columbia and Alberta, form one of the world's great fishing, canoeing and wilderness-camping regions. This area is famous for majestic, towering, snow-capped mountain ranges, vast Boreal and coastal rain forests, tundra, wild river valleys, and thousands of remote blue lakes and turbulent streams.

British Columbia, the westernmost and third largest of Canada's provinces, covers 366,255 square miles of dramatic landscape. Here are the world-renowned salmon, trout and steelhead waters of Vancouver Island and the mist-shrouded Queen Charlotte Islands. The western hemlock and sitka spruce are scattered with stands of mountain hemlock, red elder, black cottonwood and thick understories of dwarf blueberry, red huckleberry and salmonberry.

Beyond the fabled rain forests and steelhead streams of the Coast Mountains lie the rocky beaches of the Pacific Ocean, with its mild Japan Current, and countless islands, bays, spits, and inlets known as the "Inside Passage." The thousands of square miles of alpine wilderness of British Columbia's mountains offer some of the most beautiful high-country hiking in the world. The wilderness trails were blazed by Indian guides, fur traders, and explorers who opened the land west of the Great Divide before the Canadian Pacific Railway. Thousands of miles of high-country trails wind through the mountain passes, past towering, glacier-studded peaks, through lush, alpine meadows, along turbulent mountain streams and wild rivers to remote lakeshore campsites. Mount Robson Provincial Park in British Columbia offers views of fifteen glaciers in one fourteen-mile stretch. With effort, the truly interested hiker can find in Canada some of the last primitive country left on this continent, and enjoy it in well-earned solitude.

Every four years, for a three-week period in mid-October, the Adams and Little rivers are in scarlet flood as about 2,000,000 sockeye salmon return here to spawn and die. These salmon have a four-year life cycle. They are hatched here, spend a year in Shuswap Lake and migrate to the Pacific as fingerlings the next spring. In the fourth year, they leave the ocean, swim some 17 miles a day up the Fraser and Thompson Rivers into Kamloops Lake, and finally through Shuswap Lake to the Adams and Little rivers. During this 300-mile journey, their bodies change from a steely, ocean blue to the scarlet of spawning.

The high country of the Rocky Mountains is awesomely beautiful, with its alpine meadows, headwater lakes, massive glaciers, ice fields and deep valleys protected within the boundaries of Waterton Lakes, Banff, and Jasper National Parks. Alberta covers 255,285 square miles and includes the greatest topographical variety of any of Canada's provinces. Alberta has great forest reserves and mountain ranges. The tundra region of the far north is the summer range of the barren ground caribou. During the winter months they migrate into Alberta's open and sparsely-timbered rock and moss country. Mule deer, and grizzlies weighing from 400-900 pounds, inhabit the remote high country of the Rockies and the Swan Hills. The elusive mountain lion is found in the Rockies and occasionally along the river system of southern Alberta.

Yoho National Park, on the western slopes of the Rockies, boasts Takakkaw Falls, one of the most spectacular in Canada. The waterfall is formed by meltwater from the Daly Glacier in a hanging valley 1,200 feet above Yoho Valley. Garibaldi Provincial Park, 750 square miles of mountain, glaciers, rushing rivers and placid lakes, lies northeast of Squamish. The park has three recreational areas: Black Tusk, Diamond Head and Cheakamus Lake.

Saskatchewan and Manitoba make up Central Canada and are known as the Prairie Provinces. Vast stretches of prairie grasslands, parklands and great rock outcroppings are all part of the Canadian Shield. The great Churchill River is the major waterway and flows eastward through both provinces. Saskatchewan covers 251,700 square miles and Manitoba, the "keystone" state because it links the western and eastern regions of Canada, covers an area of 251,000 square miles.

Saskatchewan is canoeing country, with over 10,000 lakes ranging from tiny potholes to the deep, cold waters of Lake Athabasca in the northwest which covers 3,050 square miles and has produced giant lake trout of up to 102 pounds. Ermine, mink, river otter, striped skunk, badger, lynx, bobcat, raccoon, white-tailed jack rabbit, and snowshoe rabbit abound in this area.

Other wilderness areas include Churchill River Wilderness Canoe Country with the Sturgeon-Weir River and Frog Portage. The Far North Grayling and Caribou Country has Reindeer Lake and Clearwater River.

Manitoba contains a good portion of the Canadian Shield, which is composed of ancient Precambrian, crystalline rocks of great hardness and strength, granites, gneisses, and veins of snowy quartz. Greenstone, which is among the oldest rocks in the world, can be found in areas around Great Bear Lake and has been estimated as 2.5 billion years old. During the Quaternary period, great ice sheets covered the country of the Shield, and when the ice melted away, huge lakes remained. The Shield is believed to contain more lakes than all the rest of the world. Atikaki Wilderness has Poplar River Country and Sasaginnisak Canoe Country. The Great Northern Wilderness has Molson Lake, Molson River, Seal River, and Wolverine and Nejanalini Lake.

Eastern Canada is composed of Ontario and Quebec. Provincial Park, northwest Quebec, is one of the best organized fishing centers in Canada. Planes are still the most practical means of transport into the park, and no matter how energetically it is exploited, it will probably be effectively conserved for years to come. Other parks are Chibougamon Park, De La Verendrye Park and Algonquin Provincial Park in eastern Ontario which encompasses nearly 3,000 square miles of protected wilderness. Killarney Provincial Park covers 140 square miles of gorgeous scenery and Polar Bear Park, near Mooseonee, contains Ontario's largest concentration of polar bears. Bearded seals, walrus, arctic foxes, colonies of snow geese and blue geese, and two to three hundred caribou can also be found there.

Ontario is on the northern border of the deciduous forest area. Here and there the woods still yield a few hickory, beech and black walnut trees, but they are disappearing. Half a century ago they were plentiful, as were the sweet chestnuts. Another treasure of nature that is fast disappearing from Ontario is the mushroom, plentiful in the days when the land was tilled by horse-drawn plows.

Ontario and Quebec offer over a million square miles of boundless, remote, blue lakes and vast evergreen forests, mountain glaciers, and world-renowned fishing and canoeing areas. Within Ontario's boundaries are found some 250,000 lakes and innumerable streams. Lake of the Woods has 14,000 evergreen-clad islands.

The northern lights are luminous meteoric phenomena appearing at night in the northern hemisphere. Electrically charged particles from the sun are diverted toward the earth's magnetic poles where they collide with gases in the atmosphere – change their electrical charge. Displays are most frequent around the times of greatest sunspot activity. At full intensity the aurora will cover the entire night sky with erratic, shifting curtains of brilliant white light and dancing, curved bands of green or rose.

The Boreal forests cover three quarters of Ontario's forest land. The forests stretch in a continuous belt of varying width from Manitoba to the Quebec border north of Lake Superior. The word "Boreal" comes from Greek mythology, after Boreas, the personification of the north wind. Trees of the Boreal forest are mostly coniferous, white spruce and black spruce being the most common. Other trees include tamarack, balsam fir and jack pine.

"The long, ghostly cry of the loon, piercing the quiet of the night, is the haunting symbol of the northern lake country. The Cree Indians believed that it was the cry of a dead warrior who had been forbidden entry into heaven. Often known as the great northern diver, the loon can dive 200 feet down and swim faster than most fish. It eats its catch quickly and its bill is often empty when it returns to the surface, although ten fish might be in its stomach. If something frightens it, the loon can swim submerged with only its beak out of the water."

Another noble animal of the north is the moose. The moose population is spread over most of the province, except for the southern lowlands and the western shores of Hudson and James Bays. Moose live where coniferous forests are mingled with deciduous growth, preferring logged or burned areas where new forest growth provides a plentiful supply of browse, since they eat an average of 50 pounds a day.

Yet another beautiful animal is the lynx, a silent and solitary hunter found in the great spruce forests of Quebec. Extremely large feet, covered with thick hair, serve as snowshoes, allowing the lynx to travel easily over deep snow. Their winter coats are soft, thick and bluish-gray, usually speckled with a tinge of brown. Other animals of Quebec's forests are the snowshoe hare, beaver, wolverine, mink, river otter, bobcat, marten, and the arctic fox in the far north.

Atlantic Canada encompasses the provinces of Newfoundland, Labrador, Nova Scotia, Prince Edward Island and New Brunswick – a group commonly referred to as the Maritime Provinces. Inland, this magical area is a land of fog, mist-shrouded moors and Boreal forests, dotted with blue lakes and slashed by wild rivers. It also has gently rolling plateaus. Labrador and Newfoundland have fine salmon fishing. The Minipi River Trophy Brook Trout Western area contains magnificent country and caribou as well. The Great Northern Peninsula, Gaspé Peninsula and Lower St. Lawrence, James Bay Region, Laurentians, North Shore Fish and Game Region and Ungava Salmon and Caribou Country are some of the notable parks.

The Labrador Current brings icebergs close to parts of the Newfoundland coast in June and July. Curiously eroded ice, as high as 150 feet, looms over Twillingate's wooded houses.

Newfoundland is full of beauty. Both Terra Nova National Park and Avalon Peninsula are magnificent. Newfoundland suggests the wild west coast of Ireland, while the province of Nova Scotia lives up to its name by being, indeed, a new Scotland. The most Scottish of places west of the Hebrides, Cape Breton Island, has rocky cover and, shrouded in mist on a gray day, the pines provide dark accents which make it serene and delightful. Kilts and bagpipes are still part of the traditional culture. Cape Breton Island is considered one of the great outdoor recreation areas in North America and is world-renowned for its majestic beauty. The northern highlands, coastal cliffs, dense evergreen forests and deep-flowing, crystal-clear rivers of the island are separated from the Nova Scotia mainland by the Strait of Canso.

Cape Breton Highlands National Park encompasses 367 square miles of ancient Appalachian highlands, rugged coastal cliffs, rocky beaches, streams, lakes, Acadian forests, treeless barrens and bogs. The scenic highlands reach an altitude of 1,747 feet, the highest point in Nova Scotia, and spectacular cliffs rise to 1,000 feet above the park's western shores.

Prince Edward Island is 140 miles long and lies offshore from both Nova Scotia and New Brunswick. Fundy and Kouchiboujuac National Parks are truly splendid. The Acadian Trail winds 375 miles, and the Fundy Trail winds 190 miles, over fantastic scenic countryside.

Indeed, the term "fantastic scenic countryside," whilst not telling the whole story of Canada's natural wonders, is probably as good a way as any to describe, at least in part, the splendor of this magnificent country.

Facing page: a scene near the seaport of Churchill, in northeastern Manitoba.

Above: horses by the Yukon Territory's Kluane Lake in Kluane National Park. The Yukon River (facing page) is one of northern Canada's major waterways, and during the Klondike goldrush of the 1890s it was one of the busiest rivers in the world.

Straits and channels between a series of islands, lying up to sixty miles offshore, and the mainland form the Inside, or Inland, Passage (above), also known as the Marine Highway. Used by coastal shipping, it covers more than 1,000 scenic miles from Puget Sound, Seattle, Washington, to Skagway, Alaska. Facing page: mountains near the west coast of Vancouver Island, which itself borders part of the Inside Passage.

Above: devil's club along Mount Revelstoke's Giant Cedar Trail in Mount Revelstoke National Park, located in the Selkirk Mountains of British Columbia. Facing page: the lower montane region of Yoho National Park, on the west slopes of the Rocky Mountains in British Columbia. The name Yoho means 'How Wonderful' in the language of the Cree Indians.

Above: a mountain lake in British Columbia, a province lying almost entirely within the great mountain system, or cordillera, that stretches along the western edge of the Americas. Facing page: the boardwalk of Mount Revelstoke's Giant Cedars Trail in Mount Revelstoke National Park, British Columbia.

Facing page: Upper Campbell Lake and Buttle Lake beyond, on Vancouver Island, British Columbia. Above: Bute Inlet, mainland British Columbia.

Above: a coyote in Kootenay National Park, and (facing page) Mount Odaray Plateau Grand View in neighbouring Yoho National Park, on the western slopes of the Rocky Mountains, British Columbia.

Above: peaks near the Elaho Valley, and (facing page) an aerial view of the Rockies between Squamish and Mount Whistler, both in British Columbia.

Facing page: Wapta Falls in Yoho National Park, British Columbia, viewed from one of the logging roads in this richly-forested area. Above: sunset over Mount Revelstoke National Park, one of British Columbia's smaller parks, daubs the Canadian Rocky Mountains dusky pink.

Above: a glacier near Pemberton, and (facing page) the Bishop Glacier near the Lillooet Valley, both within British Columbia.

Above: Mount Harkin and neighbouring peaks in Kootenay National Park, British Columbia. South Beach (facing page) in Pacific Rim National Park, British Columbia, is renowned for the large amounts of driftwood left there by the tide.

Right: Bear Falls on Connaught Creek in Mount Whistler ski resort, British Columbia. Bunch berries (top) on the path to Mount Sir Donald and western anemones (above) are all part of the rich plant life of Glacier National Park, British Columbia. Facing page: a moose in Kootenay National Park, British Columbia.

The view south from the Upper Lillooet Valley across the Coast Mountains (facing page) of British Columbia, is a spectacle of peaks, glaciers and valleys, one of which forms the head of the Lillooet Glacier (above).

Facing page: Dome Point and the Asulkan Glacier seen from Abbott Ridge in Glacier National Park, British Columbia. Pacific Rim National Park comprises the rugged west coast and islands off Vancouver Island, British Columbia, and includes South Beach (above).

Above: Mount Waddington is the highest peak in the Coast Mountains of British Columbia. Garibaldi Lake (facing page) is set in the mountainous terrain of Garibaldi Provincial Park, British Columbia.

Mount Robson Provincial Park, British Columbia, preserves 200,000 hectares of mountains, valleys and waterways such as the Robson River (above). Facing page: a severe aspect of Yoho National Park, British Columbia.

British Columbia offers many such spectacular mountain scenes as the territory around
Mount Whistler (above) and Mount Waddington (facing page).

The Kananaskis River (above), a tributary of the Bow River, flows through forested slopes near Lake Louise in Banff National Park, Alberta. Facing page: the Athabasca River in Jasper National Park, Alberta.

Left: Writing-on-Stone Provincial Park in Chinook country near Lethbridge, on the Milk River, Alberta, was once a secret Indian writing ground where pictographs are inscribed in the rock. Below, bottom and bottom left: Dinosaur Provincial Park, Alberta. Facing page: the eroded hoodoos of Dinosaur Valley near Drumheller, Alberta.

Facing page: Mount Eisenhower, also known as Castle Mountain, in Banff National Park, Alberta. Above: the Canadian Rockies.

Medicine Lake (above) in Jasper National Park, Alberta, is hemmed in by the Colin Range to the north and the Maligne Range to the south. Fed by melting snow, it is full during the summer, but later in the year its water seeps through holes in the limestone bedrock to resurface in Lake Beauvert and as springs in the Maligne Canyon. Facing page: the Athabasca River, Alberta.

Above: bison grazing the prairie beneath the mountains of Waterton Lakes National Park, Alberta. Moraine Lake (facing page), at the feet of the Wenkchemna Peaks in Banff National Park, Alberta, was formed when a rock deposit, thought to be a moraine, blocked the northern end of the valley.

Astotin Lake (facing page) lies in Elk Island National Park, one of Canada's smaller parks, covering only 76 square miles, located in Alberta's Beaver Hills. It is famous for its heavily-forested, undulating land, and its wildlife, especially elk (above) and bison.

These pages: the high-peaked Rocky Mountains of Alberta.

In Alberta wheat fields (facing page) flourish where the fur trade was once the foundation of the area's economy. David Fife's hardy strain of wheat, 'Red Fife', developed in 1842, proved more than equal to the climate of the prairies and greatly aided their cultivation. Above: an Albertan lake.

Above: Vimy Ridge and Mount Richards, beyond Maskinonge Lake in Waterton Lakes National Park, Alberta. Near Drumheller, Alberta, the Red Deer River and convergent streams have eroded a trail of gullies (facing page), exposing ancient rock strata beneath modern farmland.

These pages: Lake Louise in winter. The distinctive colour of this lake is caused by the suspension of mineral-rich rock sediment in the glacier meltways which feed it, causing it to look turquoise in summer and milky-green in winter.

Peyto Lake (above) in Banff National Park, Alberta, is fed by water flowing through the Rocky Mountains from Peyto Glacier and has a milky blue colour caused by rock dust from the glacier suspended in the water of the lake. Facing page: a mountain goat and her kid.

Facing page: Stanley Peak straddles the border between Alberta and British Columbia. In the mountains of the Continental Divide, Lake Louise (above) in Banff National Park, Alberta, was known as the 'lake of the little fishes' by the Stony Indians who led Tom Wilson to it. He called it Emerald Lake, but it was later renamed for Princess Louise, the wife of Lord Lorne, Governor-General of Canada.

These pages: deer in Elk Island National Park, located in Alberta's Beaver Hills.

Facing page: a meltwater stream of the Columbia Icefield in Jasper National Park, Alberta, the largest sheet of prehistoric ice on this continent south of the Arctic. Above: Athabasca River in Jasper National Park.

Small and narrow, Moraine Lake (facing page), lying in Banff National Park, Alberta, reflects the Wenkchemna (Stony Indian for 'ten') Peaks in its waters. Above: a moose near Banff, Alberta.

The 1,496 square miles of Saskatchewan's Prince Albert National Park are representative of Canada's southern plains (above) on which the aspen forests of the south mingle with true boreal wilderness. Facing page: a pond near the park's Heart Lakes.

Facing page: a willet (Catoptrophorus semipalmatus), which breeds either on western lakes or in eastern coastal marshes, and (above) a Wilson's phalarope (*Phalaropus tricolor*), an uncommon member of the sandpiper family, which nests by prairie sloughs and ponds.

Above: grasslands in the prairie vastness yielding wheat, and (facing page) uncultivated prairies serving as pastureland.

These pages: beavers feeding and building in Prince Albert National Park, Saskatchewan. The variety of environments within Prince Albert National Park enables it to support many different kinds of animals. Northern forests form the beaver's habitat.

Facing page: a prairie rattlesnake, and (above) a ferruginous hawk of the open
Saskatchewan grasslands, which are particularly famous for their unusual birdlife.

Facing page: horses grazing the south Saskatchewan prairie. Above: sweeping clouds over Grasslands National Park in southwestern Saskatchewan, created to preserve the plants and wildlife of the original prairies.

Above: a beaver lodge beside Amiskowan Lake in Prince Albert National Park, Saskatchewan. Large forests of conifers and aspen are typical of Prince Albert National Park (facing page).

Polar bears (these pages) meet around the area of Churchill on Hudson Bay in Manitoba at the onset of winter. Enthusiasts are able to observe these usually solitary animals at this time.

By virtue of its dense, weather-proof fur and the thick, hairy soles of its feet, the polar bear (these pages) is a speedy traveller across the icy terrain it inhabits. Polar bears are hunted, but not for food, as their high vitamin A content makes them inedible, even poisonous.

Between aspen trees, the road to Lake Audy (above) curves through Manitoba's Riding Mountain National Park. Clear Lake (facing page), the largest lake in Riding Mountain National Park, is popular with water-sport enthusiasts.

Manitoba's vast open plains (above) posed an agricultural problem to early immigrant farmers through a combination of rich, heavy soil and extremes of climate. Eventually the experience that Ukranians and Russian Mennonites had of the Russian Steppes overcame this to make Manitoba one of the most productive farming areas in Canada. Facing page: a bald eagle in Riding Mountain National Park, Manitoba.

Facing page: a spring waterscape and (above) the frozen sea off Auyuittuq National Park,
formerly Baffin Island National Park, in the Northwest Territories. The park was renamed
Auyuittuq, an Inuit word meaning 'the place which does not melt', in 1975.

The First Canyon (above) on the South Nahanni River in Nahanni National Park, Northwest Territories, is enough to draw visitors to a relatively inaccessible area. Earlier travellers were lured by the prospect of gold, often to a mysterious doom. The name Nahanni is an Indian word for a legendary 'giant people over there, far away'. Facing page: smoke from a forest fire drifts across the park.

The land of the north is being constantly formed and gradually altered by glacial activity scouring great 'U' shaped canyons in underlying rock by dragging rock debris over the surface and thereby grinding still more rock into powder. This is eventually carried down to the lakes, charging them with mineral-rich colour, a result of the suspension of rock dust in the water. Pingos, great blocks of ice, form underneath the land and push upwards forming bulges in the landscape. This many-faceted glacial erosion produces spectacular landscapes (these pages).

Thunder Bay (above), Ontario, forms the inland terminus of the Saint Lawrence Seaway, capable of handling the largest ships on the lakes. Facing page: Lake of the Woods in Rushing River Provincial Park, Ontario.

Top left: the view from Castle Bluff along the north shore of Flowerpot Island in Georgian Bay Islands National Park, Ontario. Top right: rock formations above Castle Bluff. Left: 'Large Flowerpot' on Flowerpot Island, where the bunchberry (above) and one-leaf rein archis (top centre) are found. The flowerpot formations were caused by strong wave action and receding water levels. Facing page: the trail through the woods near Castle Bluff, Flowerpot Island.

Facing page: the shore of Lake Superior, and (above) the view from Horseshoe Beach looking towards Lake Superior's Pic Island and Ogilvy Point, both in Pukaskwa National Park, Ontario.

Above: the shore of Lake Superior after a storm, and (facing page) the boreal forest of the Southern Headland, on the northern shore of Lake Superior, both in Pukaskwa National Park, Ontario.

Facing page: Millbay on Lake Superior, and (above) the Rushing River Rapids in Rushing
River Provincial Park, near Lake of the Woods, both in Ontario.

Roughly half way along its course from Lake Erie to Lake Ontario, the Niagara River dramatically changes level, plunging suddenly over the rim (above) of a cliff. Niagara Falls (these pages) actually consist of two falls: the American Falls on the U.S. side of the river, and the larger Canadian, or Horseshoe, Falls.

These pages: the Laurentian Region, to the north of Montreal, in La Mauricie National Park, Quebec. This area was originally explored by trappers in canoes.

The Nell River (these pages) is a passage for salmon (above) pressing upstream towards their spawning grounds. Among the many hazards they have to navigate en route are the bears who live on seasonally easy pickings (facing page).

Facing page: the Lac en Croix Brook, running from the hills to feed one of the many lakes of
La Mauricie National Park (these pages), Quebec.

The fjord-like landscape created by the cliffs around Western Brook Pond (above), and the cataract of Bakers Brook Falls (facing page), both lie in Gros Morne National Park, Newfoundland, which is the product of four glaciation periods and the ensuing climatic erosion.

Terra Nova National Park (these pages), Newfoundland, contains some carnivorous plants, such as the pitcher plant (above), and the sundew plant (facing page). These entrap their prey and digest them by means of both enzymes and bacteria.

Red sandstone rubble litters the shore (far left) near Orby Head (below left), and (left) near Cavendish on Prince Edward Island. Below: two cormorants at Orby Head. Facing page: a piping plover protects her egg and newly-hatched chick.

The setting for Lucy Maud Montgomery's famous novel, *Anne of Green Gables*, Prince Edward Island (these pages), or 'the garden of the Gulf', is so fertile that it has been described as two huge beaches separated by potato fields, a description which in no way does justice to its great beauty and agricultural variety.

Above: the Mersey River in Kejimkujik National Park, Nova Scotia, and (facing page) the Dickson Falls in Fundy National Park, New Brunswick. Overleaf: white-tail deer in Kejimkujik National Park, Nova Scotia.